Contemporary
Papier Mâché

Colorful Sculpture, Jewelry, and Home Accessories

Gilat Nadivi

Creative Publishing international

Contemporary

Papier Mâché

Creative Publishing international

First published in 2008 by Creative Publishing international, Inc.
Creative Publishing international, Inc., a member of
Quayside Publishing Group
400 First Avenue North
Suite 300
Minneapolis, MN 55401
1-800-328-3895
www.creativepub.com

Copyright 2007 Penn Publishing Ltd.

ISBN-13: 978-1-58923-354-6
ISBN-10: 1-58923-354-9

10 9 8 7 6 5 4 3 2 1

Library of Congress Cataloging-in-Publication Data

Nadivi, Gilat.
 Contemporary papier mâché : colorful sculpture, jewelry, and home accessories /
Gilat Nadivi.
    p. cm.
 ISBN 1-58923-354-9
 1. Papier-mâché. I. Title.
 TT871.N34 2008
 745.54'2--dc22

                                                    2007042597
                                                    CIP

Book Design: Eddie Goldfine
Cover Design: Ariane Rybski
Photographs: Danya Weiner

Printed in Singapore

Contents

Introduction

Papier mâché is the perfect environmentally friendly craft, and an excellent hobby for people who love working with their hands. The name comes from the French word, *papier mâché*, meaning chewed paper. It involves using shredded or torn paper and paste to construct sturdy, lightweight articles of virtually any size or shape. Papier mâché is easy to make, as it uses simple tools and easy-to-find materials. It is easy to dry, as well; you need nothing more intricate than air!

The projects in this book use two papier mâché techniques. One technique involves shaping papier mâché pulp, which is made from shredded paper that is soaked in water, drained, and mixed with paste. This pulp resembles chewed paper or cooked oats. It is ideal for sculpting items such as beads, decorative hearts, or birds, and for adding detail to large sculptures and figurines.

The other technique involves soaking torn strips of newspaper in water, dipping them in paste, then laying them on a surface. This technique can be used to make diverse works ranging from decorative bowls to elegant chairs. Many projects in this book use both techniques—damp newspaper strips dipped in papier mâché paste to cover large surfaces, and papier mâché pulp to mold details.

All of the projects use objects that have outlived their initial purposes. In addition to newspaper, this includes empty water bottles, disposable chopsticks, empty cardboard tubes, and decorative napkins. Feel free to improvise with materials you find around your own home, and keep your eyes open the next time you gather items for the recycling box or trash bin. You never know what may find new life under a layer of papier mâché!

Ideas for these projects came from the things I see around me everyday—from elderly women lying on the beach to young people hanging out at cafés, playful animals, and colorful flowers. I am also inspired by artists such as Henri Matisse, Niki de Saint Phalle, and Joan Miró, among others, all of whom have created remarkable works of art using this versatile, tactile medium.

Papier mâché is a pleasure for artists of all ages and all levels of skill. Basic projects such as bracelets or beads are great for beginners; more experienced artists will enjoy the challenge of sculpting elaborate figurines. Papier mâché is a tactile art that is always different, always exciting. No two projects turn out alike, so prepare yourself for an adventure in paper, and enjoy!

Materials

The projects in this book use a variety of items you may never have imagined integrating into art. In most cases, the materials you need are already lying around your home, so keep your eyes peeled, and be creative! Any items you don't have on hand can be found in craft stores or online.

Acrylic paints: These are used to decorate the final work. In most projects, you'll paint a white base coat first to conceal the newspaper strips or papier mâché pulp.

Assorted recyclables: These include empty water bottles, plastic plant pots, and small boxes. Almost anything can take on new life when covered with papier mâché and a coat of colorful paint!

Beads: A few beads can add a lot of life to a papier mâché project. Imbed them in the wet papier mâché pulp or string them on a string with papier mâché beads or small figures.

Cardboard tubes: Save every cardboard tube you come across, as you never know when they may come in handy. Short tubes are great for making legs; longer tubes are perfect for supporting tall figures. Toilet papier, wrapping paper, paper towels, plastic wrap, and aluminum foil are all great sources of sturdy cardboard tubes.

Caster wheels: The kind of wheels found on office chairs are used to create mobile statues, such as Dalmatian on a Roll (see page 68). Salvage a set from an office chair that has outlived its usefulness, or pick some up at an office supply store.

Chopsticks and wooden skewers: These disposable wooden sticks are used as supports for legs and flower stems. Tape them end to end to make a longer support; tape them side by side to make a sturdier frame.

Corrugated plastic board: Thick plastic board is an excellent work surface when creating papier mâché. When your project is wet, the papier mâché sticks to the board, giving you extra stability. Once the piece is dry, it comes off the board easily.

Decorative napkins: These are used to create colorful decoupage. Look for other items that may be used for decoupage as well, such as greeting cards, wrapping paper, tissue paper, and magazines.

Hot glue and glue gun: These are used to affix strips of fabric and assorted accessories to the final project. Apply hot glue once the work is completely dry.

Masking tape: Many papier mâché projects require lots of masking tape, so be sure you have plenty on hand before you start. Save the empty cardboard rings—they are great for making bangles (see page 102)!

Mesh wire: Similar to chicken wire, this wire is used to build a sturdy yet flexible base upon which to apply papier mâché.

Modeling clay: An excellent way of adding small features such as sunglasses, shoes, and earrings is to shape them with air-drying modeling clay. Just be sure these additions are relatively small, as wet modeling clay can be quite heavy.

Newspaper: Papier mâché is a great way to recycle old newspaper. Shred it, crumple it, or rip it into strips. (Don't cut it with scissors!) For projects in which the newspaper will be visible, take extra care when selecting the newspaper. In most projects, the paper is completely covered in paint.

Paintbrushes: These are used to apply acrylic paint and varnish to the finished project. They are also used to apply wallpaper paste for decoupage.

Sculpting wire: This is used to shape the base in several projects. If you find that you have cut your wire too short for a specific project, simply twist on another piece. The wire is eventually concealed under the papier mâché, so any adjustments to the base won't be visible in the final work.

Sturdy scissors or sharp knife: Have these on hand to cut plastic board or cardboard. Don't use scissors to cut newspaper. Ripping it by hand along the grain is best.

Varnish: This is applied to painted works to protect them and add a glossy finish.

Vertical stands: Some figures are constructed on stands made of metal or wood. You can order stands from a blacksmith, or use paper towel stands. You can also make your own stand by placing a stick into a plastic cup and pouring in plaster. When the plaster sets, you'll have a sturdy stand perfect for covering with papier mâché.

Wallpaper paste: This clear paste is used to smooth papier mâché pulp as it is applied to the project. Along with white glue, it is added to soaked, shredded paper to make papier mâché pulp. It is mixed with white glue to form the paste that is used to apply strips of newspaper. Be sure to follow the manufacturers' instructions when mixing the paste.

White glue: Nontoxic paste, also known as PVA, is added to the soaked, shredded paper to make papier mâché pulp. It is mixed with wallpaper paste to form the paste that is used to apply strips of newspaper. It is also used to affix small accessories to the final piece.

White paper: Nonglossy office paper can be shredded to make papier mâché pulp. Make sure the paper is free of staples and paper clips before preparing the pulp.

Wire cutters: This sturdy tool is used to trim wires and wooden skewers. Don't substitute scissors, as this could cause the wood to splinter, or simply break the scissors.

Writing utensils: Permanent markers are used to draw patterns on corrugated plastic board; pencils are used to sketch patterns on cardboard. You may also want to sketch patterns onto the base coat of paint before painting your project.

Papier Mâché Techniques

Papier Mâché Pulp

This pulp takes a few days to make, so begin preparing it before you want to work on your project. It is excellent for sculpting delicate flowers, birds, and facial features, but can just as easily be used to cover an entire picture frame or statue. The texture is quite versatile; it can be left rough or smoothed over with wallpaper paste.

MATERIALS

- shredded newspaper or white office paper
- 2 clean buckets
- water
- immersion blender
- cotton fabric, such as old cotton shirt or cloth diaper
- large plastic bowl
- 2 to 3 cups white glue
- 2 tablespoons powdered wallpaper paste

Instructions

1 Place shredded paper in a bucket. Make sure there are no staples or paper clips.

2 Pour in water until the paper is completely immersed, and set aside to soak for two or three days. You'll know you are ready for the next step when the paper is soft and mushy.

3 Press down on the paper with your hands, and pour out excess water. Insert immersion blender and blend until the mixture becomes a watery pulp.

4 Spread cotton fabric over empty bucket and hold taut. If possible, have someone help you by holding the fabric while you pour in the pulp.

5 Pour some of the pulp onto the fabric. Twist the fabric around the pulp and squeeze tightly to drain excess liquid into the bucket. Squeeze a few more times to make the pulp as dry as possible, then transfer to a large bowl. Repeat until all of the pulp has been squeezed thoroughly and transferred to the bowl.

6 Run your fingers through the pulp, breaking it into small pieces.

9 Run your fingers through the pulp, breaking it into small pieces. Add 2 cups of white glue and wallpaper paste, and mix well. Mold the pulp with your hands; if it can hold a shape, it is ready to be used. If not, add a little more white glue and mix well.

10 The pulp can be used immediately or stored in an airtight container in the refrigerator for an indefinite period of time.

7 Add 2 cups of white glue and the powdered wallpaper paste, and mix well.

8 Mold the pulp with your hands. If it can hold a shape, it is ready to be used; if not, add a little more white glue and continue mixing.

Damp Newspaper Strips and Papier Mâché Paste

This technique involves applying strips of newspaper that have been dipped in paste. It requires little advance preparation, and is excellent for covering large surfaces. Be sure to work methodically, so that the layers of paper are applied evenly. This technique works best with newspaper; if you use colored or white paper, make sure the paper is very thin.

MATERIALS

- newspaper
- clean bucket
- water
- large plastic bowl
- 1 cup white glue
- $\frac{1}{2}$ cup prepared wallpaper paste
- small plastic bowl

Instructions

1 Rip newspaper along the grain into 2" x 8" (5 x 20 cm) strips (although the exact size depends on the project, and your preference). Place strips in bucket and pour in water until the paper is completely immersed. Set aside to soak for 30 minutes.

2 Remove strips from the bucket, squeeze out excess water, and transfer to a large bowl.

3 In small bowl, mix together white glue and wallpaper paste to make papier mâché paste.

4 To apply, dip the strips, one at a time, into the papier mâché paste, and lay on your work. Flatten the strips as you apply them to press out air bubbles.

Tip
When using this technique, apply at least two or three layers of newspaper to your project.

Tips of the Trade

Plan in advance. Papier mâché is a wet craft, and every stage takes time to dry. Even simple projects require advanced planning, as they must dry thoroughly before being painted. If you are planning to give your work as a gift, start working on it long before you want to present it.

Apply a thin layer of papier mâché paste (see page 13) to the base of projects made with newspaper and masking tape. This prevents the masking tape from coming unstuck before you apply papier mâché pulp or damp newspaper strips dipped in papier mâché paste.

Use white office paper or newspaper ONLY when making papier mâché pulp. Do not use glossy paper, as it will not break down when soaked in water. If you use colored paper, be sure it is thin.

Apply papier mâché pulp evenly. Though papier mâché is very light when dry, wet papier mâché pulp is rather heavy. If it is not applied evenly, too much weight at one end or another can cause the work to become lopsided or break.

For large projects, apply papier mâché pulp in stages. Wet papier mâché pulp is heavy. If you are sculpting something large, do so in stages, allowing the pulp to dry in between. This helps prevent breakage due to excess weight.

Dry all projects thoroughly before painting. The drying time of every project varies according to the type of papier mâché, and its thickness. In general, layers of newspaper dipped in paper mâché paste take two or three days to dry; projects made from papier mâché pulp take four or five days to dry. However, these are just guidelines, and drying times depend on various factors including the thickness of the papier mâché and the humidity of the air. Rotate your work as it dries, so that all sides are exposed to the air.

Dry projects in direct sunlight, if possible. Needless to say, if there is even the slightest chance of rain, don't risk it!

Apply a base coat of white acrylic paint to all objects before painting or applying decoupage. This gives you a neutral background which ensures that the colors you paint will turn out vibrant.

If you think it will help, sketch your design onto the base before painting. Some projects look best painted freehand; others benefit from having a sketch drawn onto the white base before painting.

Take a break. Papier mâché takes time. If you run out of patience while working on your project, simply put it aside for a while. If you are using papier mâché pulp, return the pulp to the refrigerator and allow the project to air dry. When you come back to it, your project will be sturdier and lighter.

Fun for all ages. Papier mâché is a great activity for artists of any age. The materials are simple, the mess is minimal, and the products are safe.

Work from inspiration. Photographs, fabrics, and real objects are excellent sources of inspiration for papier mâché projects. If you are building an elephant, for example, keep a photograph of one nearby. When painting flowers, the real thing is often the best source of guidance.

Ready to Start

Working with papier mâché is soothing and relaxing, but only if everything you need is at hand while you work. Before you begin any papier mâché project, prepare your work area as follows:

Lay a corrugated plastic board on your work surface. When your project is wet, it will stick to the board; but once it is dry it will be easy to remove.

Rip and soak strips of newspaper. If the project requires damp newspaper strips, rip plenty in advance and soak them in water for about 30 minutes before you begin.

Rip strips of masking tape. If the project requires you to tape crumpled pieces or strips of newspaper, you'll want the masking tape ready before you start sculpting. Place several strips along the edge of your work table (or any other appropriate surface), and replenish as necessary.

Prepare pastes. If your project requires wallpaper paste or papier mâché paste, prepare it in advance and keep at your work area.

Sketch your project. Drawing a picture of the item you plan on making can provide guidance as you work.

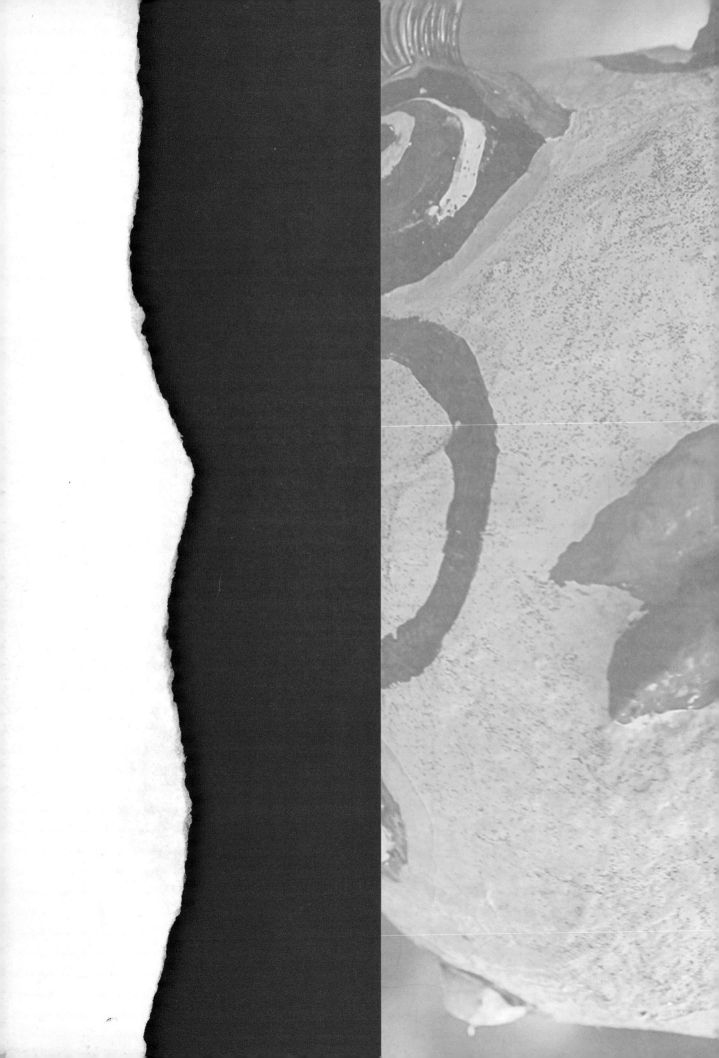

Projects

Urban Redhead

Height: 16" (41 cm)

If you always dreamed of dying your hair fire engine red—but never dared actually doing so—here is an excellent chance to live vicariously.

MATERIALS

- sculpting wire
- wire cutters
- newspaper
- masking tape
- corrugated plastic board
- papier mâché pulp (see page 10)
- wallpaper paste
- acrylic paint and paintbrushes
- varnish
- hot glue and glue gun
- red faux fur
- red and white checkered fabric

Instructions

1 Cut a 60" (153 cm) piece of wire and fold it in half. Measure about 1" (2.5 cm) from the folded end and twist a couple of times to form a loop. Open the loop to make a circle for the head—the twisted area is the neck. Before continuing, doublecheck to make sure you like the proportions.

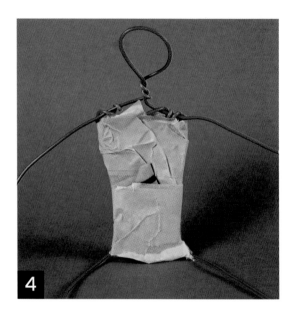

4 Continue wrapping the torso, taking care to apply several strips of newspaper between the legs to separate them. Wrap some masking tape tightly near the bottom of the torso to form a waist.

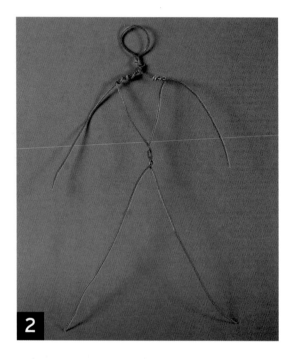

2 To make the arms, measure 8" (20 cm) on either side of the neck and cut the wires. Wrap the cut pieces of wire on either side of the twist, about 1" (2.5 cm) from the neck, to form shoulders. Draw these wires downwards and twist together about 4" (10 cm) below the neck to form the waist. The wires extending below the waist form the base for the legs. Bend each wire about 1" (2.5 cm) from the bottom to form feet.

3 Begin wrapping the figure with strips of newspaper and masking tape. Start by wrapping the torso to form a rectangular body over the triangular base.

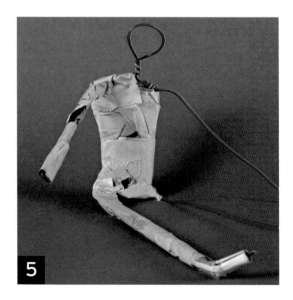

5 Wrap the arms with newspaper and masking tape, taking care that they are even in size and length. Wrap smaller strips of newspaper at the bottom, for hands. Wrap newspaper and masking tape around the legs. Bend the legs at the bottom to form shoes, and secure them with masking tape.

6

9

6 Crumple newspaper into a ball and stuff it into the loop at the top to form the head. Secure the head with thin strips of newspaper and tape, shaping the ball into an egg shape.

7 When the figure is completely covered, arrange the arms and legs into your desired position.

8 Set the figure on a plastic board and apply papier mâché pulp to the bottom—the hips and thighs—to stabilize it. The figure will stick to the board when the pulp is wet, but will peel off easily once the pulp has dried.

9 Continue applying papier mâché pulp to the rest of the figure. Be sure to apply pulp evenly to the top and bottom of the figure as you work–too much wet pulp on one area can make the figure lopsided or cause it to topple. Gently apply wallpaper paste with the palm of your hand to smooth the pulp as you work.

10 Sculpt the nose and mouth with pulp, and make gentle indents for the eyes. Use the pulp to shape hands, shoes, and other details. Set aside to dry for four or five days.

11 When the figure is completely dry, apply a base coat of white acrylic paint. Allow the base coat to dry, then paint as desired and apply a coat of varnish. Use hot glue to affix faux fur to the head for hair, and fabric around the waist for the skirt.

Cool Guy

Height: 16" (41 cm)

This figure (see photo page 18) is inspired by life in the city. Hanging out on the weekend; people-watching; waiting for something to happen. He makes a perfect match for Urban Redhead but doesn't mind living the single life, either.

MATERIALS

- sculpting wire
- wire cutters
- newspaper
- masking tape
- corrugated plastic board
- papier mâché pulp (see page 10)
- wallpaper paste
- acrylic paint and paintbrushes
- varnish
- white glue
- stud
- short chain

Instructions

1 Cut a 60" (153 cm) piece of wire and fold it in half. Measure about 1" (2.5 cm) from the folded end and twist a couple of times to form a loop. Open the loop to make a circle for the head—the twisted area is the neck. Before continuing, doublecheck to make sure you like the proportions.

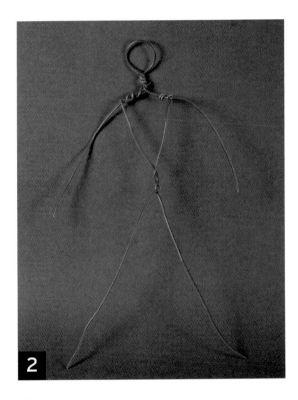

3 Begin wrapping the frame with strips of newspaper and masking tape. Start by wrapping the shoulders and torso to form a rectangular body over the triangular base.

2 To make the arms, measure 8" (20 cm) on either side of the neck and cut the wires. Wrap the cut pieces of wire on either side of the twist, about 1" (2.5 cm) from the neck, to form shoulders. Draw these wire pieces downwards and twist together about 4" (10 cm) below the neck to form the waist. The wires extending below the waist form the base for the legs. Bend each wire about 1" (2.5 cm) from the bottom to form feet.

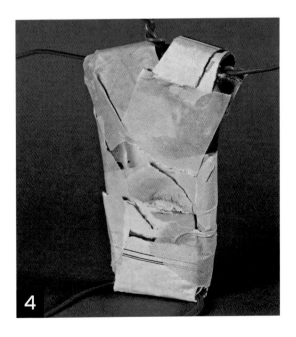

4 Continue wrapping the body, taking care to apply several strips of newspaper between the legs to separate them.

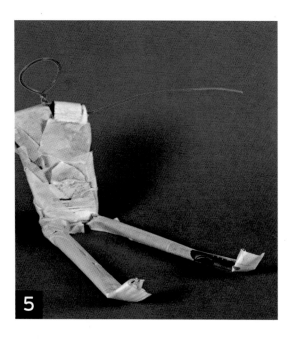

5

5 Tear long strips of newspaper, wrap them around the legs, and secure them with masking tape. Bend the legs upwards near the bottom to make shoes, and secure them with masking tape.

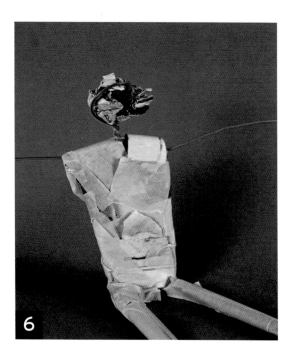

6

6 Crumple some newspaper into a ball and stuff it into the loop at the top to form the head. Secure it with strips of newspaper and tape, shaping the ball into an egg shape.

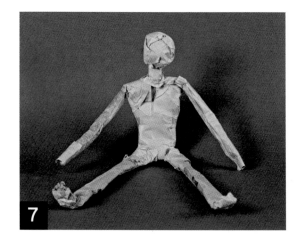

7

7 Wrap the arms with newspaper and masking tape, taking care that they are even in size and length. Wrap smaller strips of newspaper at the bottom, for hands.

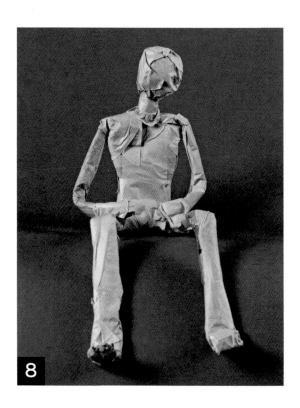

8

8 When the figure is completely covered, arrange the arms and legs into your desired position.

9 Set the figure on a plastic board and apply papier mâché pulp to the bottom—the hips and thighs—to stabilize it. The figure will stick to the board when the pulp is wet, but will peel off easily once the pulp has dried.

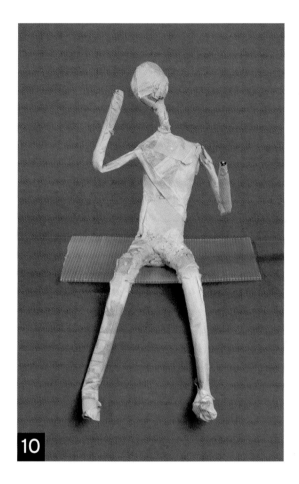

10

10 Continue applying papier mâché pulp to the rest of the figure. Be sure to apply pulp evenly to the top and bottom of the figure as you work—too much wet pulp on one area can make the figure lopsided or cause it to topple. Gently apply wallpaper paste with the palm of your hand to smooth the pulp as you work.

11

11 Sculpt the nose and mouth with pulp, and make gentle indents for the eyes. Use the pulp to shape hands, shoes, and other details. Set aside to dry for four or five days.

12 To make the hat, shape a wide band of papier mâché pulp around the head. Top with a smaller amount of pulp shaped into a cylinder. Set aside to dry for four or five days.

13 When the figure is completely dry, apply a base coat of white acrylic paint. Allow the base coat to dry, then paint as desired and apply a coat of varnish. Use white glue to affix a stud for the belt buckle, and attach a chain around the neck.

Pretty Lady in a Red Dress

Height: 15" (38.4 cm)

Wrap one leg of this figure around a vertical support to make a dancer that really stands out from the crowd. Follow the same technique but arrange the legs in front of the figure to making a lounging lady.

MATERIALS

- sculpting wire
- wire cutters
- 12" (30.7 cm) vertical stand
- newspaper
- masking tape
- papier mâché pulp (see page 10)
- wallpaper paste
- acrylic paint and paintbrushes
- varnish

Instructions

1 Cut a 50" (130 cm) piece of wire and fold it in half. Measure about 1" (2.5 cm) from the folded end and twist a couple of times to form a loop. Open the loop to make a circle for the head—the twisted area is the neck. Before continuing, doublecheck to make sure you like the proportions.

2 To make the arms, measure 8" (20 cm) on either side of the neck and cut the wires. Wrap the cut pieces on either side of the twist, about 1½" (4 cm) from the neck, to form shoulders. Draw the wires downwards and twist together about 4" (10 cm) below the neck to form the waist. The wires extending below the waist form the base for the legs.

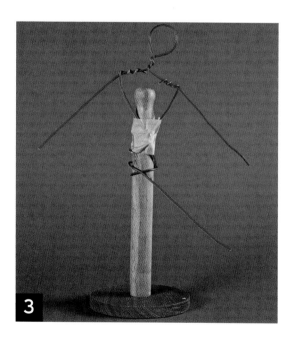

3 Position the figure in front of the stand and secure it with masking tape. Twist one of the legs around the stand—you won't be needing it, since the stand functions as the base for this leg—and wrap the other leg once around the stand, allowing it to extend outwards.

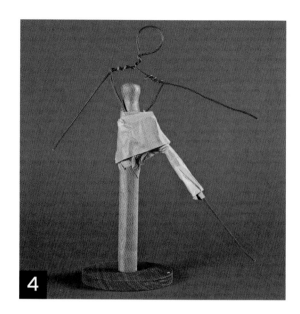

4 Begin wrapping the frame with strips of newspaper and masking tape. Use enough masking tape to ensure that the figure is securely fastened to the stand. Take care to apply several strips of newspaper between the legs to separate them. You can start wrapping newspaper around the top of the extended leg now, too.

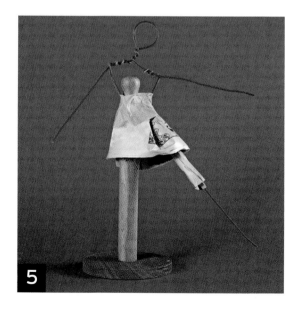

5 Wrap several layers of newspaper and masking tape around the hips to form the skirt.

6

7

6 Crumple some newspaper into a ball and stuff it into the loop at the top to form the head. Secure it with strips of newspaper and tape it, shaping the ball into an egg shape. Form hands and feet by wrapping smaller pieces of newspaper and masking tape. Wrap the rest of the figure with newspaper and masking tape, and remember that everything must be sized in relation to the stand. This is the widest part of the base of your figure, so be sure to wrap the other areas—especially the other leg—so that they are proportionate.

7 Once the figure is completely covered, arrange the arms and the extended leg into position.

8 When you are satisfied with the shape and proportions of the figure, begin applying papier mâché pulp. Be sure to apply pulp evenly to the top and bottom of the figure as you work—too much wet pulp on one area of the figure can make it lopsided or cause it to topple. Gently apply wallpaper paste with the palm of your hand to smooth the pulp as you work.

9 Sculpt the nose and mouth with pulp and make gentle indents for the eyes. Use the pulp to shape the hair, bosom, hands, and other details. Set aside to dry for four or five days.

10 When the figure is completely dry, apply a base coat of white acrylic paint. Allow the base coat to dry, then paint as desired. Apply a coat of varnish to finish.

Bathing Beauty

Height: 12" (30.7 cm)

This figure was inspired by the women I see on the beach, chatting away as if they haven't a care in the world. (And maybe they really don't!) The base for this figure is made from crumpled newspaper held together with masking tape.

MATERIALS

- newspaper
- masking tape
- damp newspaper strips and papier mâché paste (see page 13)
- corrugated plastic board
- permanent marker
- sturdy scissors or sharp knife
- modeling clay
- acrylic paints and paintbrushes
- varnish

Instructions

1 To make the torso, crumple newspaper into a 12" (30.7 cm) pear shape and wrap it with masking tape to secure it. The bottom of the pear is the torso; it should be considerably wider than the top.

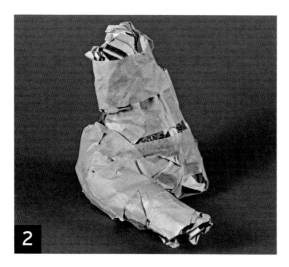

2 Prepare a leg by crumpling newspaper into another 12" (30.7 cm) pear shape, this one considerably slimmer than the previous one. Secure it with masking tape and position it so that the widest part of this leg runs alongside the torso. The slimmer part of the leg—the calf and the foot—should jut forward. Wrap it with masking tape to secure it.

3 Make a second leg similar in size and shape to the first one and attach it on the other side of the torso. Position this leg so that it crosses the first leg at the knee, and wrap it with masking tape to secure it.

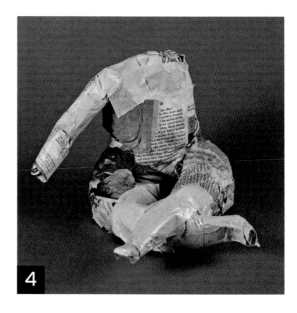

4 To make an arm, roll newspaper into a 7" (18 cm) cylinder and attach it at the top of the torso with masking tape. Bend it at the elbow and wrap it with masking tape to secure it.

5 Repeat step 4 to make the other arm and attach it on the other side of the torso, taking care to attach it at the same height on the body, although at a slightly different angle.

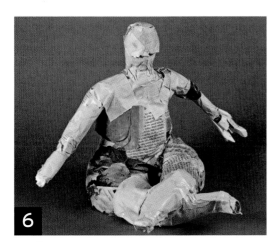

6 Form the head by crumpling some newspaper into a 1 1/2" (4 cm) ball and wrapping it with masking tape. Make a neck by rolling a cylinder of newspaper, and secure it with masking tape. Affix the head and neck to the torso with masking tape. Before continuing, doublecheck to make sure you like the proportions.

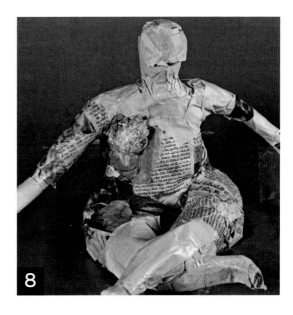

8 To form the chest, crumple a single strip of damp newspaper, dip it in the papier mâché paste, and press it onto the body. If the paper slides down, lay the figure on its back while building up the chest.

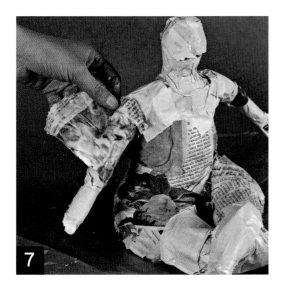

7 Start at the hip area and begin applying layers of damp newspaper strips dipped in papier mâché paste to the figure. Once the base of the figure is stable, move on to the arms and upper body, applying layers of newspaper dipped in papier mâché paste.

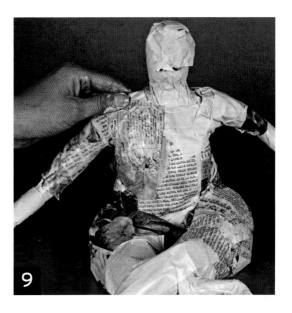

9 Apply layers of damp newspaper dipped in papier mâché paste over the crumpled paper to smooth the surface and secure the chest in place.

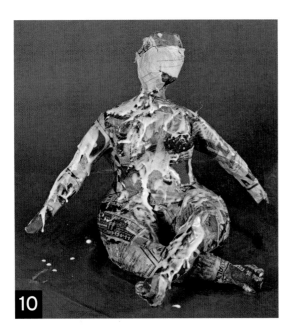

10 Add crumpled bits of paper dipped in the paste to create contours at the hips, feet, and other curvaceous areas, then cover them with layers of newspaper dipped in the paste to secure and smooth. When the figure is fully covered, apply papier mâché paste with your hands, and set it aside to dry for two or three days.

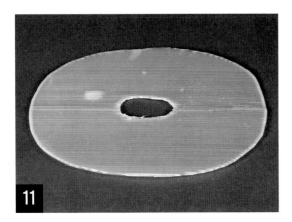

11 To make the hat, draw an 8" (20 cm) circle on the plastic board and cut out. In the middle of the circle, cut a hole that is large enough to fit over the crown of the head, but not so large that it causes the hat to slip over the face. If in doubt, make the hole too small and enlarge as necessary.

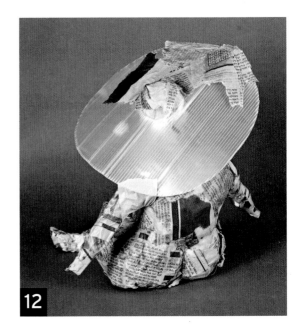

12 Place the hat on the head and adjust it to the right angle. Apply damp newspaper strips dipped in papier mâché paste to the hat rim. Set it aside to dry for two or three days.

13 Shape shoes, sunglasses, earrings, and other accessories directly onto the figure using modeling clay, and set aside to dry. When the figure is completely dry, apply a base coat of white acrylic paint. Allow the base coat to dry, then paint as desired. Apply a coat of varnish.

Tip
Doublecheck the size of all the elements as you work and adjust proportions by adding more layers of newspaper and tape, as necessary.

Court Clown with Rings

Height: 25" (64 cm)

One of the classic figures in European art and entertainment, the black and white harlequin, is perfect for recreating in papier mâché. I recommend working from a photograph of a real harlequin, and sketching the features onto your white base before applying the acrylic paints (see photo page 36).

MATERIALS

- sculpting wire
- wire cutters
- masking tape
- newspaper
- 20" (51.2 cm) vertical stand
- damp newspaper strips and papier mâché paste (see page 13)
- papier mâché pulp (see page 10)
- wallpaper paste
- modeling clay
- acrylic paints and paintbrushes
- varnish

Instructions

1 Cut a 65" (166 cm) piece of wire and fold it in half. Measure about 1" (2.5 cm) from the folded end and twist a couple of times to form a loop. Open the loop to make a circle for the head—the twisted area is the neck. Before continuing, doublecheck to make sure you like the proportions.

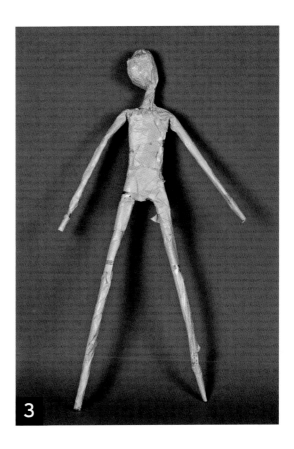

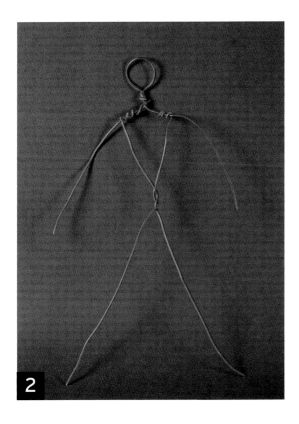

2 To make the arms, measure 8" (20 cm) on either side of the neck and cut the wires. Wrap the cut pieces on either side of the twist, about 1 ½" (4 cm) from the neck, to form shoulders. Draw the wires downwards and twist together about 5" (12.8 cm) below the neck to form the waist. The wires extending below the waist form the base for the legs.

3 Wrap the figure with strips of newspaper and masking tape. Begin by wrapping the torso to form a rectangular body, then wrap the arms and legs. Take care to apply several strips of newspaper between the legs to separate them. When wrapping the legs, make one slimmer than the other, as the slimmer leg will be attached to the metal stand, which adds volume. Crumple some newspaper into a ball and stuff it into the loop at the top to form the head. Secure it with strips of newspaper and tape, shaping the ball into an egg shape and tilting it at an angle.

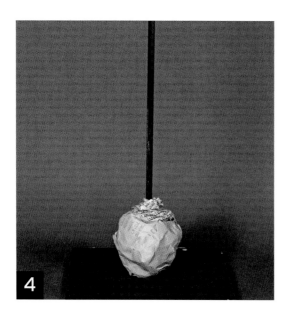

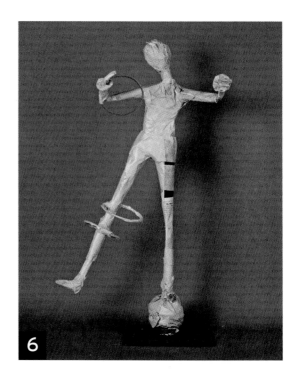

4 Crumple strips of newspaper into a ball and cover it with masking tape. Affix it to the base of the stand with masking tape.

6 Arrange the arms and hands in the desired position. Cut small pieces of wire and shape into rings; attach them securely with masking tape.

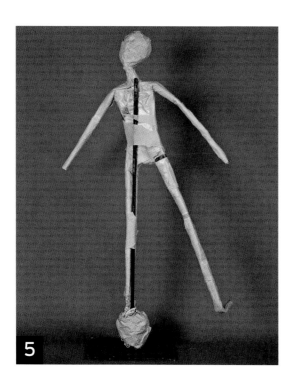

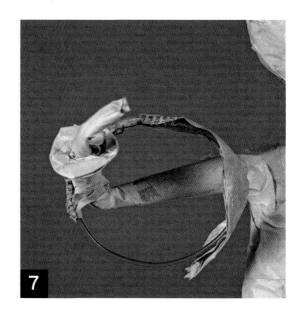

5 Bend each leg at the bottom to form feet, and check to make sure the legs are even. Position the figure so that the slimmer leg is in front of the stand and on top of the ball. Attach the figure securely to the stand using masking tape.

7 Use damp newspaper strips dipped in papier mâché paste to wrap the rings, and to strengthen the connection between the figure and the rings. Set it aside to dry for two or three days.

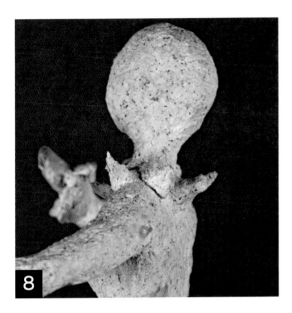

8 Apply papier mâché pulp all over the figure. Gently apply wallpaper paste with the palm of your hand to smooth the pulp as you work. Sculpt the collar by forming small cones of papier mâché pulp all around the neck.

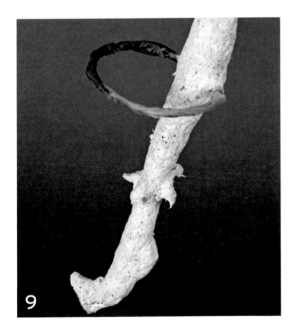

9 Form shoes with papier mâché pulp, and draw the ends upwards to a point. Sculpt rounded cuffs on the sleeves and triangular cuffs at the ankles, and set it aside to dry for four or five days.

10 When the figure is completely dry, use modeling clay to shape buttons and other details directly onto the figure, and set it aside to dry.

11 Apply a base coat of white acrylic paint. Allow the base coat to dry, then paint as desired. Apply a coat of varnish to finish.

Dancer in a Blue Ruffled Skirt

Height: 15" (38.4 cm)

The skirt in this project is made by layering folded pieces of newspaper dipped in papier mâché paste into a fluffy fan. Add shiny sequins and fluffy faux fur hair to create a character that is a definite show stopper!

MATERIALS

- sculpting wire
- wire cutters
- masking tape
- newspaper
- 12" (30.7 cm) vertical stand
- papier mâché pulp (see page 10)
- wallpaper paste
- damp newspaper strips and papier mâché paste (see page 13)
- acrylic paints and paintbrushes
- white faux fur
- small blue sequins
- hot glue and glue gun

Instructions

1 Cut a 60" (153 cm) piece of wire and fold it in half. Measure about 1" (2.5 cm) from the folded end and twist a couple of times to form a loop. Open the loop to make a circle for the head–the twisted area is the neck. Before continuing, doublecheck to make sure you like the proportions.

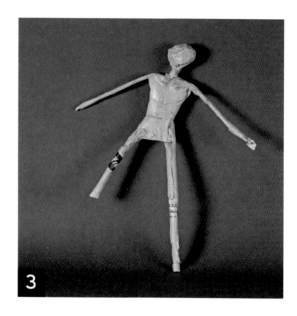

3 Begin wrapping the figure with strips of newspaper and masking tape. Start by wrapping the torso to form a rectangular body, then wrap the arms and legs. When wrapping the legs, take care to wrap several strips of newspaper between the legs to separate them. Wrap fewer strips around the shorter leg than the longer leg, as the stand will add width once attached.

2 To make the arms, measure 8" (20 cm) on either side of the neck and cut the wires. Wrap the cut pieces of wire on either side of the twist, about 1 1/2" (4 cm) from the neck, to form shoulders. Draw the wires downwards and twist together about 4" (10 cm) below the neck to form the waist. The wires extending below the waist are the legs. Cut the right leg so that it is significantly shorter than the left leg. The right leg will be attached to the stand, which will make up for the missing length.

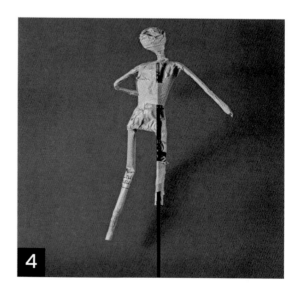

4 Using masking tape, attach the figure securely to the stand at the back and along the leg.

5

8

5 Once the figure is securely attached, arrange the arms and legs into your desired position. Raise the left leg and bend it at the knee; position the left hand under this leg to support it. This support is important for keeping the figure balanced while applying the papier mâché pulp, and while the pulp dries.

6 Begin applying papier mâché pulp along the left leg only, just until the hip. Gently apply wallpaper paste with your palm to smooth the pulp as you work. Set it aside to dry for two or three days. Do not apply pulp to the hand supporting the leg, as this isn't its final position.

7 Once the left leg is dry, position the left hand above the leg. Apply papier mâché pulp to the rest of the figure now, taking care to sculpt the right leg so that it is even with the left leg. Be sure to apply pulp evenly to the figure as you work—too much wet pulp on one area of the figure can make it lopsided or cause it to topple.

8 Sculpt the nose and mouth with pulp, and make gentle indents for the eyes. Use the pulp to shape hands, the bosom, high-heeled shoes, and other details. Don't forget to form the bloomers that will be visible under the skirt. Set it aside to dry for four or five days.

9

9 When the figure is completely dry, begin making the layered skirt. Tear several 12" (30.7 cm) strips of newspaper, in widths ranging from about 1" (2.5 cm) to 4" (10 cm). Apply papier mâché paste to both sides of the newspapers using a paintbrush.

10 Fold each strip of newspaper into a fan, making the pleats about 1" (2.5 cm) wide. Lay the figure on its back and start affixing the front of the skirt. Affix the widest fan at the waist with a little papier mâché paste. Affix a narrower fan over top, and continue affixing fans—from widest to narrowest—until you have a full skirt at the front of the figure. Set it aside to dry for two or three days.

11 When the front of the skirt is dry, turn the figure on its side and apply fans of newspaper, again from widest to narrowest, along the back. Set it aside to dry for two or three days.

12 When the figure is completely dry, apply a base coat of white acrylic paint. Allow the base coat to dry, then paint as desired. Use hot glue to affix faux fur for the hair and sequins for the bodice.

PHTHALOCYANINE BLUE ●●●

ACRYLIC COLOUR

Sally: Leader of the Tribe

Height: 3' (91.5 cm)

This striking figure is painted with a single matte color, making the texture of the pulp and the detail of the sculpting particularly noticeable.

MATERIALS

- newspaper
- masking tape
- cardboard wrapping paper tube
- damp newspaper strips and papier mâché paste (see page 13)
- wooden skewers
- papier mâché pulp (see page 10)
- wallpaper paste
- wire cutters
- acrylic paints and paintbrushes

Instructions

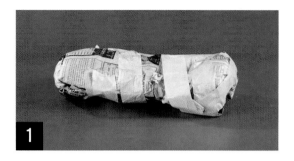

1 Make the torso by folding several sheets of newspaper into a 7" x 10" (18 x 25.6 cm) rectangle. Wrap it with masking tape to secure it.

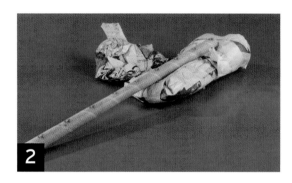

2 Support the torso by taping the cardboard tube lengthwise along the back. The tube serves both as the base of the neck and to support the head, so make sure it extends several inches above the top of the torso.

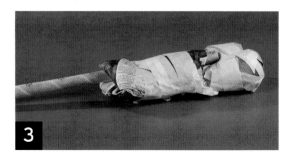

3 Wrap several pieces of newspaper and masking tape around the torso and cardboard tube to secure it.

4 To make a leg, roll several pieces of newspaper into a long cylinder and wrap it securely with masking tape. Allow some pieces of newspaper to extend beyond the top of the cylinder. (You'll use these to affix the leg to the torso.) Bend the cylinder near the middle to form a knee, and near the bottom to form a foot.

5 Repeat step 4 to make a second leg, taking care that the legs are similar in length and width. Affix the legs at the bottom of the torso with masking tape.

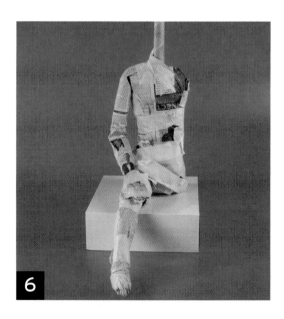

6 Make an arm in a similar manner as the legs, by rolling several pieces of newspaper into a long cylinder and wrapping it securely with masking tape. Bend the cylinder to form the elbow and hand.

7 Repeat step 6 to make a second arm, taking care that the arms are similar in length and width. Affix the arms securely at the shoulders with masking tape.

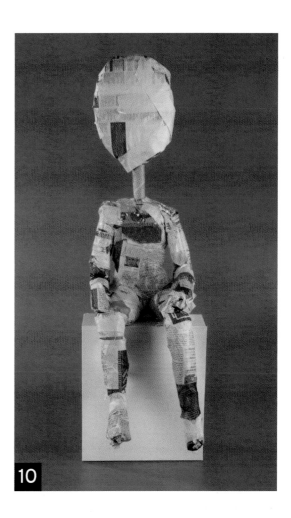

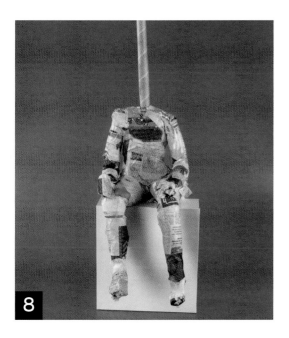

8 Your figure now has two arms, two legs, a torso, and a sturdy spine-like cardboard tube. Position the arms and legs in the desired position, and wrap with masking tape to ensure everything is securely affixed.

9 To make the head, lay a large sheet of newspaper on your work surface and fold it in half. Crumple several pieces of newspaper into balls and gather them together in the middle of the newspaper. Wrap the sheet around the balls to form a thick disk about 8" (20 cm) long and secure it with masking tape.

10 Place the head in front of the tube, leaving an exposed area below for the neck. Make sure you are satisfied with the length of the neck, then secure the head with masking tape. Add layers of newspaper and masking tape to strengthen the head and shoulder area. Before continuing, doublecheck to make sure you like the proportions.

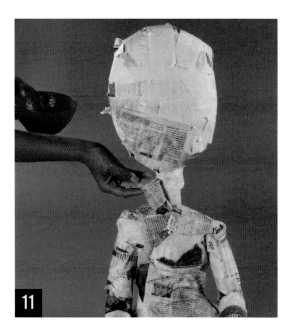

11

11 Begin applying damp newspaper strips dipped in papier mâché paste to the neck area first, to strengthen the connection here and make it particularly secure, then continue all over the figure. Set it aside to dry for two or three days.

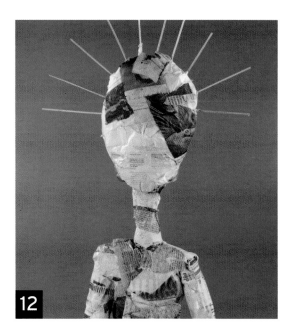

12

12 To make a base for the hair, insert wooden skewers in an arc at the top of the head.

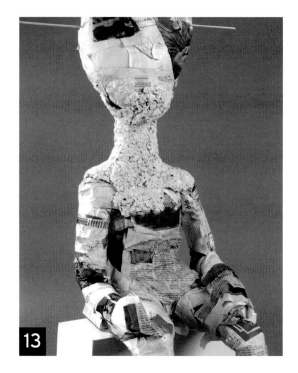

13

13 Apply papier mâché pulp to the neck, chin, and shoulders, to ensure that this area is particularly strong. Gently apply wallpaper paste with the palm of your hand to smooth the pulp as you work. Set it aside to dry for four or five days.

14 Now apply papier mâché pulp all over the figure, adding more pulp to the neck and face, as well as to the arms, legs, and torso. Be sure to apply the pulp evenly at the top and bottom of the figure so that it is balanced as you work. Set it aside to dry for four or five days.

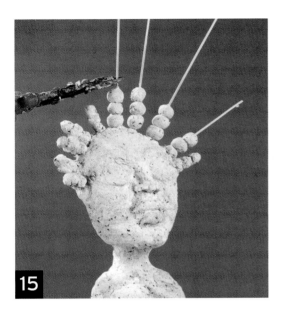

15 When the figure is completely dry, sculpt the facial features with papier mâché pulp, and smooth them with wallpaper paste. To make the hair, roll several balls of papier mâché pulp and carefully press them onto each skewer. Use wire cutters to cut away excess skewer extending beyond the top ball, and set it aside to dry for four or five days.

16 Doublecheck to make sure you are satisfied with the proportions. Apply papier mâché pulp to the areas that need building up, such as the bosom, hands, feet, and face. Set it aside to dry.

17 When the figure is completely dry, apply a base coat of white acrylic paint. Allow the base coat to dry, then paint as desired.

Happy Sea Turtle

Final dimensions: 28" x 10" (71.7 x 25.6 cm)

Real turtles are generally a staid green color, but working in papier mâché provides an excellent opportunity to add a little pizzazz. This turtle is quite large, but don't be daunted by its size—it's very friendly!

MATERIALS

- newspaper
- masking tape
- corrugated plastic board
- permanent marker
- sturdy scissors or sharp knife
- damp newspaper strips and papier mâché paste (see page 13)
- papier mâché pulp (see page 10)
- wallpaper paste
- acrylic paint and paintbrushes
- varnish

Instructions

1 To make the body, lay a large sheet of newspaper on your work surface. Fold it in half so it has a double layer. Crumple several pieces of newspaper into balls and place them in the middle of the sheet of newspaper. Fold the newspaper up and around the balls to form a thick disk, and secure it with masking tape.

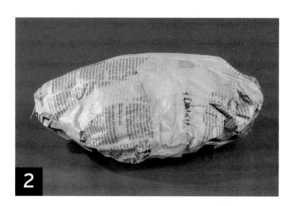

2 Repeat the technique described in step 1 to make a shell for the turtle, only place a few more crumpled balls of newspaper in the middle so that the disk is thicker and more rounded.

3 To make the head, crumple several pieces of newspaper into a ball and secure it with masking tape. Fold a sheet of newspaper several times to form a thick rectangle and affix it to the ball with masking tape to make the neck.

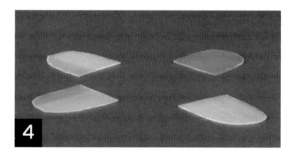

4 Draw two oblong shapes on plastic board. Cut out the shapes, then cut each shape in half widthwise to make four feet.

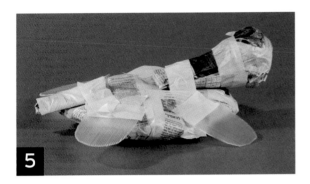

5 To assemble these pieces, place the thicker disk on your work surface so that the rounded side faces down. Position the feet on top of the disk so that the curved edges are oriented outwards and downwards, and secure them with masking tape. Place the neck and head at one end and secure them with masking tape. Roll a small cylinder of newspaper for a tail, and secure it at the opposite end.

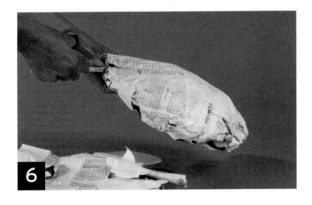

6 Lay the remaining disk on top, with the rounded side up. Note the location of the neck and cut an opening in the top disk so that it lays flat on the bottom disk.

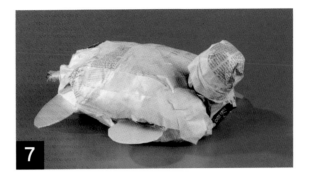

7 Wrap masking tape around the two disks to hold everything in place. Apply layers of damp newspaper strips dipped in papier mâché paste to the turtle's body, neck, and head. Set it aside to dry for two or three days.

8 When the turtle is completely dry, apply papier mâché pulp all over the top of the turtle, including the feet. Use the pulp to form eyes and a mouth. Gently apply wallpaper paste with the palm of your hand to smooth the pulp as you work. Set it aside to dry for four or five days.

9 When the top of the turtle is completely dry, turn over and apply papier mâché pulp to the bottom. Set it aside to dry for four or five days.

10 When the turtle is dry, apply a base coat of white acrylic paint. Allow the base coat to dry, then paint as desired. Apply a coat of varnish to finish.

Ella
the Elegant Elephant

Final dimensions: 15" x 6" (38 x 15.4 cm)

You may never have a chance to see an elephant in the wild, but that's no reason not to let your imagination run free with this project. I suggest keeping a photograph of a real elephant close by when sculpting the body.

MATERIALS

- newspaper
- masking tape
- 4 toilet paper tubes
- sculpting wire
- wire cutters
- corrugated plastic board
- permanent marker
- sturdy scissors or sharp knife
- damp newspaper strips and papier mâché paste (see page 13)
- papier mâché pulp (see page 10)
- wallpaper paste
- acrylic paints and paintbrushes
- varnish
- pair of artificial eyelashes
- white glue

Instructions

1 Prepare the body by crumpling newspaper into a 10" (25.6 cm) egg shape. Wrap it with masking tape to secure.

2 Flatten the paper tubes and fold them in half lengthwise. Wrap masking tape around each tube to secure it.

3 Before affixing the legs, decide how you want to orient the body. Use masking tape to attach one flattened tube at every corner on the bottom of the body. Apply the masking tape generously, as you want the legs to be secure.

4 To make the head, crumple newspaper into an 8" (20 cm) ball and wrap it with masking tape. Cut a 4" (10 cm) piece of wire for the trunk, bend it into a U shape, and tape it securely onto the head with masking tape.

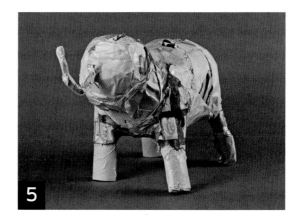

5 Affix the head to the body with masking tape. Make sure the connection is strong, as you don't want it to loosen before the papier mâché is applied. Wrap the trunk with newspaper and masking tape to add volume.

6 Draw two large ears onto the plastic board. Be sure to include a small flap along the inner edge of each ear—this is the area that will be taped to the head.

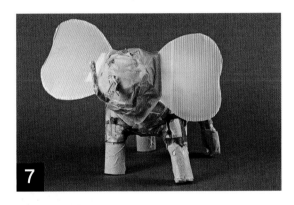

7 Cut out the ears and affix them on either side of the head using masking tape. Be sure to apply the masking tape to both the front and back of each ear.

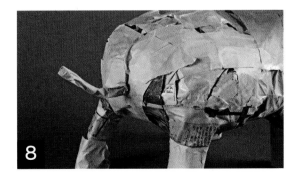

8 Cut a 1¹/₂" (4 cm) piece of wire for the tail and affix it at the back end of the elephant. Bend it into the desired position and wrap it with newspaper and masking tape.

9 Apply layers of damp newspaper strips dipped in papier mâché paste to the elephant. Begin at the connection between the head and the body. Apply several layers to secure the area where the ears are joined. Set it aside to dry for two or three days.

10 Once the elephant is completely dry, begin applying papier mâché pulp all over it. Gently apply wallpaper paste with the palm of your hand to smooth the pulp as you work.

11 Sculpt the face and mouth with pulp, and make gentle indents for the eyes on either side of the trunk. Thicken the base of the trunk, and the feet as well. Set it aside to dry for four or five days.

12 When the elephant is completely dry, apply a base coat of white acrylic paint. Allow the base coat to dry, then paint as desired. Apply a coat of varnish. Affix artificial eyelashes using a little white glue.

Lovely Lanky Giraffe

Final dimensions: 10" x 60" (25.6 x 153.6 cm)

Tall, colorful, and elegant, this graceful giraffe comes with her very own patch of grass.
I dressed her in colorful striped socks, but these lanky legs are a perfect canvas for any
design or pattern.

MATERIALS

- newspaper
- masking tape
- sculpting wire
- wire cutters
- 21 chopsticks
- damp newspaper strips and papier mâché paste (see page 13)
- papier mâché pulp (see page 10)
- wallpaper paste
- acrylic paints and paintbrushes
- varnish
- hot glue and glue gun
- ceramic tile
- piece of artificial grass
- sturdy scissors or sharp knife

Instructions

1 To form the body, tightly roll several pieces of newspaper into an 8" (20 cm) long cylinder and wrap it with masking tape to secure it.

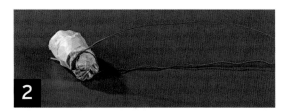

2 Make a pair of legs by cutting a 60" (154 cm) piece of wire and folding it in half. Wrap the wire around one end of the body by drawing it upwards and over the cylinder, so that equal lengths of wire hang over each side. Tie a knot in the wire at the top of the body, then draw one end of wire through the loop beside the knot to strengthen the connection. Bring the ends down on either side of the body to form legs. Repeat with another wire at the other end of the body to form a second pair of legs.

3 Make supports for each leg in the following manner: Line up two chopsticks end to end, so that they overlap by about 1" (2.5 cm). Repeat with two more chopsticks, and lay them beside the first pair of chopsticks. Wrap masking tape around the joint where all four chopsticks meet to form a thick support about 17" (44 cm) long. Repeat to make three more supports, taking care to make them all the same length.

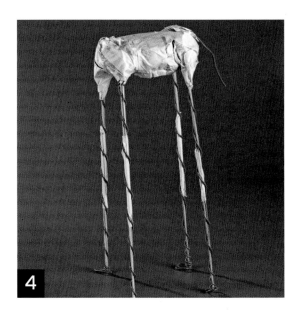

4 Secure the supports to the giraffe by placing one end of each support against the body and wrapping the wire that forms the legs around the supports to secure them in place. Bend excess wire at the bottom to form feet. Be sure to orient the feet in the same direction for each leg. To make the tail, affix a 3" (7.6 cm) piece of wire at the back of the body with masking tape and bend it into the desired position.

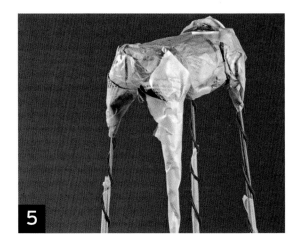

5 Wrap strips of newspaper and masking tape at the joints between the body and legs, and at the tops of the legs, to reinforce these areas.

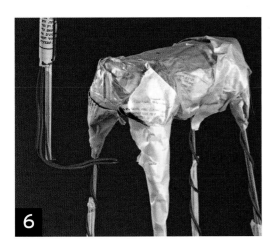

6 To make the neck, join four chopsticks together as you did to make the leg supports (see step 3). Cut a 58" (150 cm) piece of wire and wrap around the neck support, allowing 4" (10 cm) of wire to extend from the bottom of the neck. Fold this wire at a 90° angle and secure it under the body of the giraffe with masking tape. Wrap strips of newspaper and masking tape around the neck to add strength and volume. Roll a ball of newspaper and secure it to the top of the neck to form the head.

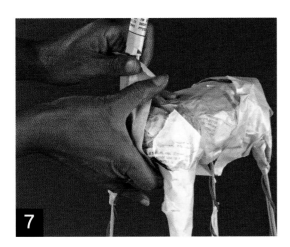

7 Reinforce the neck's connection to the body by wrapping it with several strips of newspaper and masking tape. Before continuing, doublecheck to make sure you like the proportions.

8 Start at the connections between the legs and the body and begin applying layers of damp newspaper strips dipped in papier mâché paste. Cover all of the giraffe with layers of newspaper dipped in papier mâché paste. Set it aside to dry for two or three days.

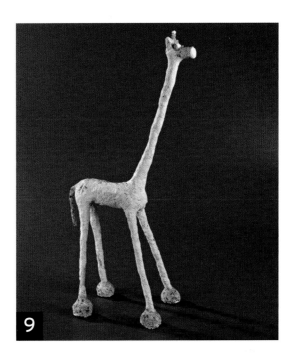

9 Apply papier mâché pulp all over the giraffe. Gently apply wallpaper paste with the palm of your hand to smooth the pulp as you work. Form a ball of pulp on the top of each foot, and sculpt a snout on the head. Use the pulp to shape triangular ears and round eyes. Cut two 2" (5 cm) pieces of a chopstick, and press them into the pulp between the ears to make horns. Set it aside to dry for one week.

10 When the giraffe is completely dry, apply a base coat of white acrylic paint. Allow the base coat to dry, then paint as desired. Apply a coat of varnish. Use hot glue to affix the giraffe to the ceramic tile. Cut the artificial grass so that it fits around the giraffe's legs, then affix it to the tile with hot glue.

Big Beautiful Blowfish

Final dimensions: 3" x 7" (7.6 x 18 cm)

As diverse as tropical fish, papier mâché fish can be any size, shape, or color. Make a lone fish for displaying on a single string, or assemble a school of them into a mobile.

MATERIALS

- balloon
- damp newspaper strips and papier mâché paste (see page 13)
- small plastic plant pot
- papier mâché pulp (see page 10)
- wallpaper paste
- wooden skewer
- acrylic paints and paintbrushes
- varnish
- pair of artificial eyelashes
- white glue
- nylon string

Instructions

1 Blow up a balloon until it is about 7" (18 cm) long, or as long as your fish. Don't inflate the balloon too much, as this makes it more fragile when applying the papier mâché.

2 Apply layers of damp newspaper strips dipped in papier mâché paste all over the balloon. Work carefully, as you don't want the balloon to pop.

3 Set it aside to dry for two or three days, rotating periodically so that the papier mâché dries evenly on all sides.

4 When the work is completely dry, apply several more layers of damp newspaper strips and papier mâché paste. Set it aside to dry for two or three days, rotating periodically.

5 When the second layer of papier mâché is completely dry, prop up the balloon on a plastic plant pot and apply papier mâché pulp to the exposed area. Gently apply wallpaper paste with the palm of your hand to smooth the pulp as you work. Set it aside to dry for four or five days.

6

7

7 When the work is completely dry, sculpt eyes, lips and other features with papier mâché pulp. One end of the balloon is pointier than the other, so sculpt the tail at this end. Add small balls along the sides and fins along the top. Gently insert a wooden skewer through the middle fin (to create a hole for the string to go through later). Set it aside to dry for three or four days. Twist the skewer inside the fin periodically so that the pulp doesn't stick.

6 When dry, rotate the piece in the plant pot and apply papier mâché pulp to the other end. Set it aside to dry thoroughly.

8

8 When the fish is completely dry, remove the skewer and apply a base coat of white acrylic paint. Allow the base coat to dry, then paint as desired. Apply a coat of varnish, and affix artificial eyelashes using a little white glue. Draw a piece of nylon string through the hole in the fin.

Dalmatian on a Roll

Final dimensions: 15" x 12" (38.4 x 30.7 cm)

For people who don't want the responsibility of walking a real dog (and even for those who do), this project makes a great pet. With a wheel under each paw, this attractive canine can almost take itself for a walk!

MATERIALS

- newspaper
- masking tape
- sculpting wire
- wire cutters
- damp newspaper strips and papier mâché paste (see page 13)
- papier mâché pulp (see page 10)
- wallpaper paste
- acrylic paints and paintbrushes
- varnish
- hot glue and glue gun
- 4 caster wheels (such as the type used on office chairs)

Instructions

1 To form the body, tightly roll several pieces of newspaper into a cylinder that is about 10" (25.6 cm) long. Wrap it with masking tape to secure it.

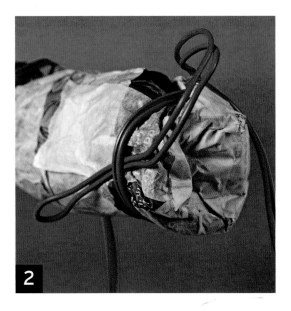

2 Make a pair of legs by cutting a 50" (128 cm) piece of wire and folding it in half. Wrap the wire around one end of the body by drawing it upwards and over the body, so that equal lengths of wire hang over each side. Tie a knot in the wire at the top of the body, then draw one end of wire into the loop beside the knot to strengthen the connection. Bring the ends down on either side of the body to form legs, and fold them up at the bottom to even up the legs and make paws.

3 Repeat step 2 with another wire at the other end of the body to form a second pair of legs. Ensure that all four legs are even.

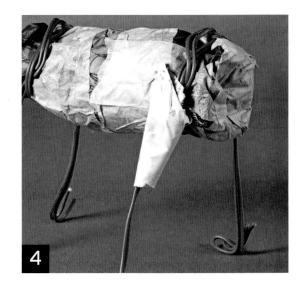

4 Wrap strips of newspaper and masking tape at the joints between the body and legs, and at the top of each leg to reinforce those areas. Form a neck by rolling newspaper into a thick cylinder, and secure it with masking tape. Crumple newspaper into a ball to form a muzzle and affix it to the top of the neck with masking tape. Attach the neck and muzzle using masking tape.

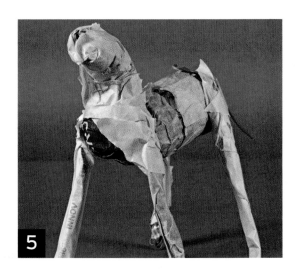

5 Wrap the legs, muzzle, and neck with several strips of newspaper and masking tape to add volume and stability. Before continuing, doublecheck to make sure you are satisfied with the proportions.

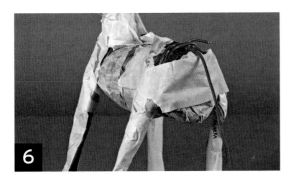

6 Cut an 8" (21 cm) piece of wire for the tail and secure it to the body by twisting it onto the wire that supports the dog's hind legs. Bend the tail into the desired position.

7 Check to make sure that the dog is stable. Double check the muzzle to make sure it is firmly attached. This is also the time to make sure that the paws are large enough to accommodate the caster wheels.

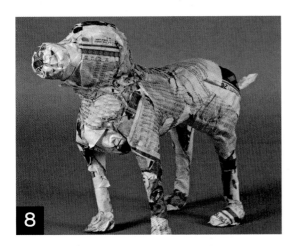

8 Apply layers of damp newspaper dipped in papier mâché paste all over the dog. To form features such as the nose and cheeks, crumple a single strip of damp newspaper, dip it in the papier mâché paste, and press it onto the dog. Apply layers of damp newspaper dipped in papier mâché paste over the crumpled paper to smooth the surface and secure it. Don't forget to cover the tail and paws. Set it aside to dry for two or three days.

9 Apply papier mâché pulp all over. Gently apply wallpaper paste with the palm of your hand to smooth the pulp as you work. Use the pulp to create details such as a chubby toes and a curly tail, and to sculpt the eyes, mouth, and tongue. Build the ears in stages since the weight of too much wet pulp could cause them to break. Shape the top half of the ears first, then set the work aside to dry for three or four days. Apply more papier mâché pulp afterwards to finish the ears. Set it aside to dry for four or five days.

10 When the dog is completely dry, apply a base coat of white acrylic paint. Allow the base coat to dry, then paint as desired. Apply a coat of varnish. Affix a caster wheel onto the bottom of each paw using hot glue.

Forever Yours Flowers

Length: 20" (51 cm)

Create a vibrant flower that never wilts, won't die, and doesn't need water. I suggest using real flowers (or color photographs) for inspiration while painting.

MATERIALS

- sculpting wire
- wire cutters
- 2 chopsticks
- newspaper
- masking tape
- damp newspaper strips and papier mâché paste (see page 13)
- papier mâché pulp (see page 10)
- wallpaper paste
- acrylic paints and paintbrushes
- varnish

Instructions

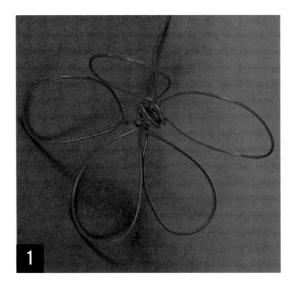

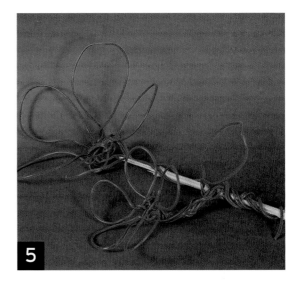

1 Cut a 50" (128 cm) piece of wire and make a loop at one end using about 4" (10 cm) of wire. Twist the end of the wire firmly to secure the loop. This loop is the first petal on your flower, and the twisted area is the flower center.

2 Move 4" (10 cm) down the wire and make a second loop, similar in size, that is twisted at the same point in the flower. Repeat to make a third loop, twisting it at the flower center as well.

3 Repeat to make five petals around the center. Strengthen the center by wrapping it several times with wire.

4 You now have a five-petal flower on a 30" (78 cm) stem of wire that extends from the flower center. Fold the wire in half to double it up, or twist it around another piece of wire, to form a sturdy stem.

5 Cut another piece of wire and make a second flower that is a little smaller than the first flower. Line up two chopsticks end to end, so that they overlap by about 1" (2.5 cm), and secure with masking tape. Twist the stems of the flowers together and wrap around the double chopstick to make a long, sturdy stem. Make a leaf or two by forming a loop in the middle of an 8" (20 cm) piece of wire and twisting it onto the chopsticks.

6 Cover each petal separately by wrapping it with strips of newspaper and masking tape. Take care that each petal is wrapped tightly, so the shape is defined. Make small balls of newspaper and affix them to the center of each flower with masking tape. Wrap the leaves and stem with layers of newspaper and masking tape as well.

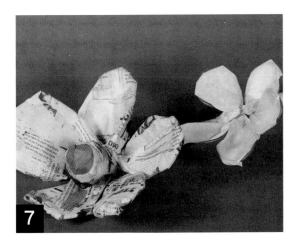

7 Apply layers of damp newspaper strips dipped in papier mâché paste to the leaves, petals, flower centers, and stem. Set it aside to dry for two or three days.

8 When the flower is completely dry, apply papier mâché pulp to the stem to strengthen it. Gently apply wallpaper paste with the palm of your hand to smooth the pulp as you work. Set it aside to dry for three or four days. Rotate the flower as it dries, so that the stem dries evenly.

10 Allow the base coat to dry, then paint as desired. Apply a coat of varnish to finish.

9 When the flower is completely dry, apply a base coat of white acrylic paint.

Picture Frame: Fit for a King

Final dimensions: 9" x 12" (23 x 30.7 cm)

These projects are created on ready-made frames. This means you can save yourself the trouble of building frames from scratch and invest all of your creative energies in decorating.

MATERIALS

- 7" x 9$\frac{1}{2}$" (18 x 24 cm) wooden picture frame
- permanent marker
- corrugated plastic board
- permanent marker
- sturdy scissors or sharp knife
- papier mâché pulp (see page 10)
- wallpaper paste
- acrylic paints and paintbrushes
- varnish

Instructions

1 Draw the contoured edge of the frame onto the plastic board and cut it out. If you want the frame to be symmetrical, cut the right side of the frame first, then trace the contours to make the left side. Cut a few teardrop shapes for placing at the top of the frame.

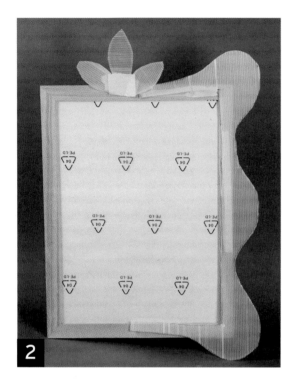

2 Remove the backing and glass from your frame (so they don't get covered in papier mâché pulp as you work). Affix the plastic cutouts securely to the back of the wooden frame with masking tape.

3 Apply papier mâché pulp to the front of the frame. Sculpt contours as desired, and gently apply wallpaper paste with the palm of your hand to smooth. Set it aside to dry for four or five days.

4 When the frame is completely dry, turn it over and apply papier mâché pulp to the back. Take care to reinforce the area where the wood and plastic meet. Set it aside to dry for four or five days.

5 When the frame is completely dry, apply a base coat of white acrylic paint. Allow the base coat to dry, then paint as desired. Apply a coat of varnish to finish.

Picture Frame: Distinctly Decoupage

Final dimensions: 6" x 8" (15.4 x 20 cm)

MATERIALS

- 5" x 7" (12.8 x 18 cm) wooden picture frame
- papier mâché pulp (see page 10)
- wallpaper paste
- acrylic paints and paintbrushes
- decorative napkins

Instructions

1 Remove the backing and glass from your frame (so they don't get covered in papier mâché pulp as you work) and place the frame right side up on your work surface. Apply papier mâché pulp to the front of the frame, building it up and sculpting contours as desired. Gently apply wallpaper paste with the palm of your hand to smooth the pulp as you work. Set it aside to dry for four or five days.

2 When the frame is completely dry, apply a base coat of white acrylic paint.

3 To apply decoupage, separate the sheets of a decorative napkin so that you are working with the printed sheet only. Cut the sheet into strips and lay onto the frame. Use a paintbrush to apply wallpaper paste, brushing from the center of the strip outwards in order to press out crinkles and air pockets. Set it aside to dry.

The Hanging Garden

Final dimensions: 31" x 20" (80 x 51 cm)

The base for this project is a large iron hanger with five evenly spaced hooks along the bottom, and one hook at the top. I ordered the hanger from a blacksmith, but you can build something similar by affixing hooks to a regular hanger.

MATERIALS

- iron hanger
- damp newspaper strips and papier mâché paste (see page 13)
- papier mâché pulp (see page 10)
- wallpaper paste
- acrylic paints and paintbrushes
- varnish

Instructions

1 Apply layers of damp newspaper strips dipped in papier mâché paste all over the hanger. Take care to cover each of the hooks, and to wrap the hanger so that both the front and back are covered in papier mâché. Set it aside to dry for two or three days.

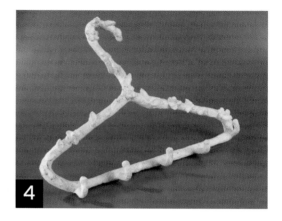

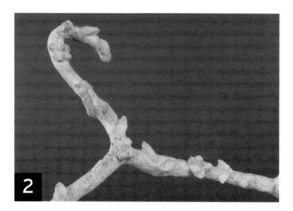

2 When the hanger is dry, cover the front with papier mâché pulp, taking care to cover the hooks as well. Use the papier mâché pulp to form flowers, bees, leaves, and other decorations. Apply wallpaper paste with the palm of your hand to smooth it. When the front of the hanger is covered, set it aside to dry for four or five days.

3 When the hanger is dry, turn it over and apply papier mâché pulp to the back. Set it aside to dry completely.

4 When the hanger is completely dry, apply a base coat of white acrylic paint.

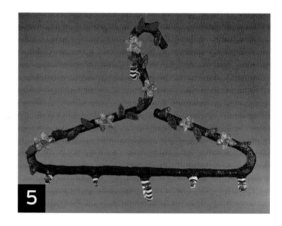

5 Allow the base coat to dry, then paint as desired. Apply a coat of varnish to finish.

Japanese-style Bowl

Final dimensions: 23" x 10" (58.8 x 25.4 cm)

Create an elegant bowl using nothing more complicated than a large bowl and a few toilet
paper tubes. Make a simpler (though no less striking) version by leaving out the legs (see
photo page 87).

MATERIALS

- large bowl
- plastic wrap
- papier mâché pulp (see page 10)
- wallpaper paste
- 3 toilet paper tubes
- newspaper
- masking tape
- acrylic paints and paintbrushes
- varnish

Instructions

1 Lay the bowl upside down on your work surface and cover it completely with plastic wrap.

2 Apply papier mâché pulp evenly across the convex surface of the bowl, taking care to make the pulp at least ¼" (0.6 cm) thick all around. This is important for ensuring that the bowl will be sturdy and usable. Gently apply wallpaper paste with the palm of your hand to smooth the pulp. Set it aside to dry for four or five days.

3 When the outside is completely dry, carefully separate the papier mâché bowl from the bowl you used as a mold. The interior of the papier mâché bowl will still be wet, so set it aside to dry for four or five more days.

4 When the bowl is dry, prepare the legs by flattening the toilet paper tubes and folding them in half lengthwise. Wrap them with masking tape to secure them. Crumple newspaper to form three small balls and tape one ball to the bottom of each tube. Turn the bowl upside down and position the legs on the bottom of the bowl. Check to make sure the legs are even–if not, trim as necessary. When you are sure the bowl sits stably on the legs, secure them in place with masking tape.

5 Apply papier mâché pulp to the legs of the bowl, and to the connection between the legs and the bowl. Form a ball at the bottom of each leg with pulp. Gently apply wallpaper paste with the palm of your hand to smooth the pulp as you work. Set aside to dry for four or five days.

6 When the bowl is completely dry, stand it on its legs and shape a thick rim using papier mâché pulp. Sculpt two birds on the rim, and set it aside to dry.

7 When the bowl is completely dry, apply a base coat of white acrylic paint. Allow the base coat to dry, then paint as desired. Apply a coat of varnish to finish.

Golden Throne with Parrot

Final dimensions: 24" x 41" (61 x 104 cm)

Who says thrones are only for royalty? Follow the steps in this project to make a decorative golden throne from nothing fancier than a simple plastic lawn chair.

MATERIALS

- corrugated plastic board
- plastic lawn chair
- permanent marker
- sturdy scissors or sharp knife
- hot glue and glue gun
- newspaper
- masking tape
- damp newspaper strips and papier mâché paste (see page 13)
- papier mâché pulp (see page 10)
- wallpaper paste
- acrylic paints and paintbrushes
- plastic bag
- gold spray paint
- varnish

Instructions

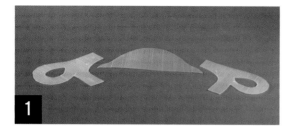

1 Place the plastic board behind your chair and draw a background, as desired. If you want the chair to be symmetrical, cut the right side of the background first, then trace the contours to make the left side. Draw a different shape for the middle of the chair and cut it out.

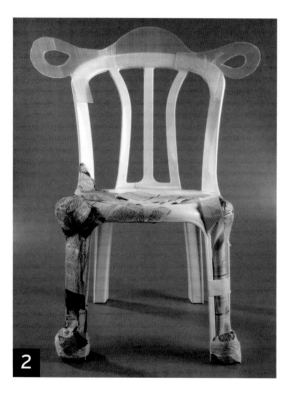

2 Affix the background to the chair with hot glue. Crumple pieces of newspaper into balls and affix them securely to the top and bottom of each leg using masking tape. Apply layers of damp newspaper strips dipped in papier mâché paste all over the legs of the chair, including the balls at the top and bottom of each leg.

3 Wrap the rest of the chair with damp newspaper strips dipped in papier mâché paste. Don't forget to cover the plastic background, and the inside of the legs. Set it aside to dry completely for two or three days.

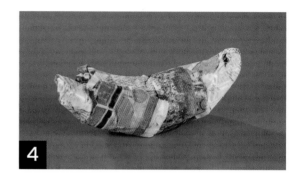

4 You can prepare the bird while waiting for the chair to dry. First, roll newspaper into a banana shape and secure with masking tape.

5 The bird's tail is made of two "feathers." To make the top feather, cut a rectangular piece of plastic board and trim one short so that it is rounded. To make the bottom feather, fold newspaper into a rectangle, and cut one end into a point.

6 Affix the plastic feather first, so that the rounded end juts upwards, in the opposite direction of the curve of the body. Position the newspaper feather between the plastic feather and the body, and secure it with several pieces of masking tape.

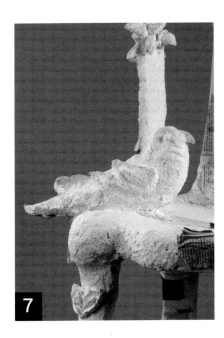

8 Apply papier mâché pulp to the seat and legs next. Use the pulp to shape forms such as flowers and leaves along the chair. Set it aside to dry for four or five days.

9 When the chair is completely dry, apply a base coat of white acrylic paint. Cover the bird with a plastic bag and spray the chair with gold spray paint. Set it aside to dry.

10 When the gold paint is dry, remove the bag from the bird and paint as desired. Apply varnish to finish.

7 When the chair is completely dry, affix the bird to the edge of the seat using hot glue. When the glue has dried, apply the papier mâché pulp. Begin by applying pulp to the connection between the bird and the chair, as you want to strengthen this area. Apply pulp all over the bird, using it to sculpt a beak, wings, and other details. Gently apply wallpaper paste with the palm of your hand to smooth the pulp as you work.

Stylish Stiletto

Final dimensions: 12" x 4" (30.7 x 10 cm)

Kick up your heels with this elegant shoe. A little more challenging than some other projects, this project is worth the effort for anyone who loves footwear. As for the height of the heel—make it as high as you dare!

MATERIALS

- wooden potato masher with a round head
- mesh wire, 20" x 20" (51 x 51 cm)
- sturdy scissors
- sculpting wire
- masking tape
- chopsticks
- newspaper
- damp newspaper (comics) strips and papier mâché paste (see page 13)
- damp strips of red paper
- small plastic flower
- white glue
- sequins

Instructions

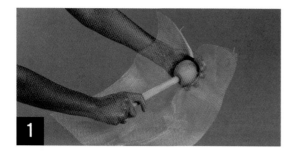

1 Make the heel first by pressing the round head of the masher into the middle of the mesh wire, about 2" (5 cm) from one edge. Sculpt the mesh around the round head to form a ball.

2 Lift the heel upwards while pressing down at the opposite end of the mesh to form the arch of the shoe. (This is the time to decide just how high you want to make the stiletto.)

3 Press down at the bottom of the arch to form the toe area of the shoe.

4 Draw the mesh on either side of the arch upwards to form the sides of the shoe.

5 Now you are ready to shape the tip. As with the height of the heel, it's up to you how dramatic you want to make the point. Form the tip by drawing the sides of mesh together on a diagonal, so that the mesh overlaps in the front area of the shoe. When you are satisfied with the dimensions, trim off the excess mesh.

6 Fold the cut edge of the mesh inwards along the opening of the shoe so that the edge of the shoe is rounded and smooth.

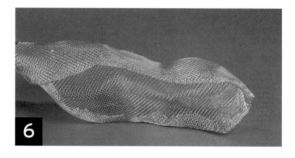

7 Twist the mesh at the front of the shoe to define the tip. Trim away excess mesh.

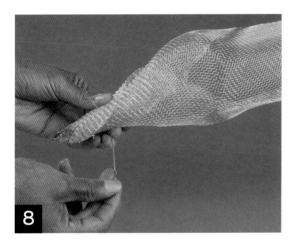

8 Wrap a piece of sculpting wire securely around the tip of the shoe to hold the two sides together.

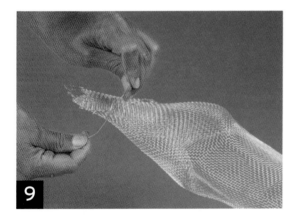

9 Weave the wire through the holes in the mesh to ensure that the hold is secure and tie in a knot.

10 To prepare the stiletto heel, hold the shoe upright and measure the distance between the heel and your work surface. Cut a chopstick to this length and wrap it with a piece of mesh wire to form a cone shape. Weave a piece of wire through the wire mesh to secure it.

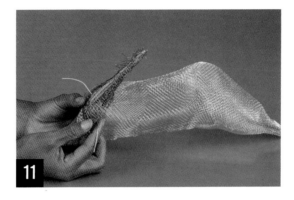

11 Position the stiletto heel with the wider side of the cone flush against the heel of the shoe. Double check to make sure the heel rests stably on your work surface. Draw a long piece of wire through the wire mesh of the shoe and the stiletto heel to secure the two together.

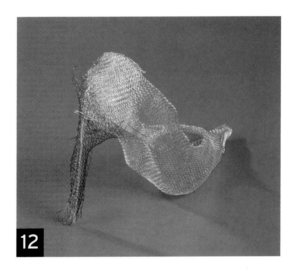

12 Wrap the wire several times through both pieces to make sure they are firmly connected.

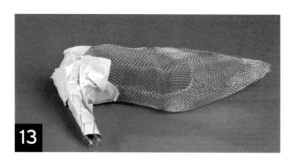

13 Begin wrapping the shoe with strips of newspaper and masking tape at the heel area, ensuring that the stiletto heel is securely attached.

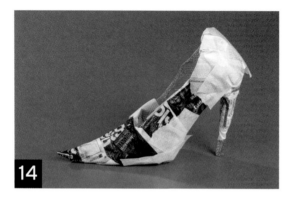

14 Continue wrapping with newspaper and masking tape, taking care to wrap the shoe tightly so that the tip remains sharply pointed.

15 When all of the shoe and heel has been wrapped, begin applying layers of damp newspaper strips dipped in papier mâché paste. Remember that these strips will be visible in the final piece, so choose the them carefully.

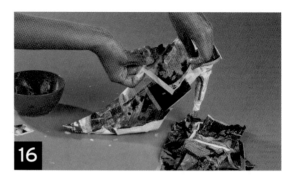

16 Be sure to cover the entire shoe with papier mâché. Don't forget to apply papier mâché to the bottom of the heel, the sole, and the inside of the shoe. Set it aside to dry for two or three days.

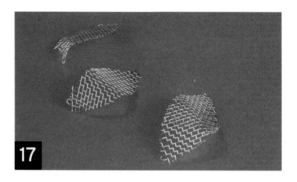

17 Prepare the flower while waiting for the shoe to dry. Begin by cutting wire mesh into several leaf-shaped petals.

18 Form a curve in each of the petals, and bring them together in a flower shape. Weave a small piece of sculpting wire through all of the petals to connect them.

19 Wrap the petals with pieces of masking tape. Cover each petal with layers of damp red paper strips dipped in papier mâché paste. Set it aside to dry for two or three days.

21 When the shoe is completely dry, affix the red flower to the shoe with a little white glue. Add a few sequins to finish.

20 Affix the plastic flower to the middle of the papier mâché flower with a little white glue.

Elegant Lace Jewelry Holder

Height: 14" (36 cm)

This small sculpture can hold your favorite necklace, pair of earrings, or bracelet. Fancy yet functional, no one would ever guess that it's made from a plastic bottle and some sand!

MATERIALS

- sand or small rocks
- small plastic bottle
- sculpting wire
- wire cutters
- newspaper
- masking tape
- papier mâché pulp (see page 10)
- wallpaper paste
- 2 iron hooks
- acrylic paints and paintbrushes
- decorative napkins
- small plastic flower
- white glue

Instructions

1

3

1 Pour sand into a plastic bottle until it is about half full.

2 Cut a 20" (51 cm) piece of wire and fold it in half. Measure about 2" (5 cm) from the fold and twist it several times to form a loop. Open the loop to make a circle for the head—the twisted area is the neck.

3 Draw the wire to the left and right of the twist to form shoulders, then bend and draw downwards. This is the frame for your figure, so make sure you are satisfied with the proportions. Wrap one end of wire around the bottle to support the figure, and press the other end inside the bottle.

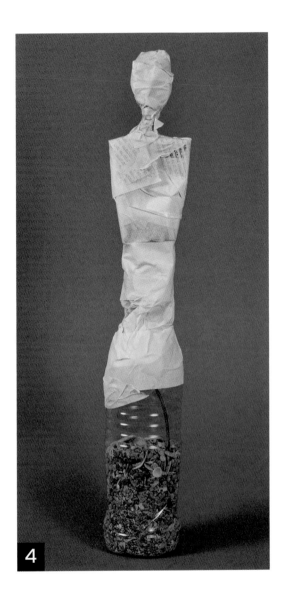

4

6

6 Carefully insert hooks on either side of the bottle, just below the shoulders, and orient them upwards. Apply papier mâché pulp over the entry point of the hooks to secure them. Set it aside to dry for four or five days.

4 Crumple newspaper into a ball and stuff it into the loop at the top to form the head. Secure it with strips of masking tape, shaping the ball into an egg shape. Wrap strips of newspaper and masking tape around the figure, taking extra care at the hip area, to ensure that the figure is securely affixed to the plastic bottle.

7 When the figure is completely dry, apply a base coat of white acrylic paint. Allow the base coat to dry.

5 Apply papier mâché pulp to the entire figure (including the bottle). Gently apply wallpaper paste with the palm of your hand to smooth it. Build contours for the hips and chest, and add extra pulp at the bottom of the bottle if you want a flared skirt.

8 To apply decoupage, separate the sheets of a decorative napkin so that you are working with the printed sheet only. Wrap the sheet around the figure to form a dress. Use a paintbrush to apply wallpaper paste, brushing it carefully from the center of each sheet outwards to press out crinkles and air pockets. Set it aside to dry. Paint on finishing touches, and affix the plastic flower at the top of the dress with white glue.

Decoupage Bangle

Final Dimension: Made to fit

Who would have thought empty masking tape rings could be so attractive? Save the rings from masking tape you use on the papier mâché projects in this book and follow these simple steps to make striking bangles of any color or design.

MATERIALS

- masking tape ring
- sharp knife
- masking tape
- papier mâché pulp (see page 10)
- wallpaper paste
- white acrylic paint and paintbrushes
- decorative napkins, newspaper comics, wrapping paper

Instructions

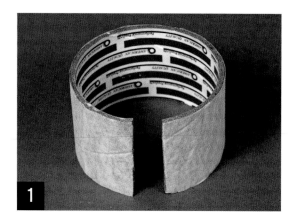

1 Make a cut in the ring and draw it around your wrist. Press the ends together to determine the size you want for your bangle. You want it to be large enough to fit comfortably over your hand, but not so large that it falls off. Take into account that the papier mâché pulp on the inside of the bangle will make it about ¼" (6 mm) smaller. Cut off the overlap.

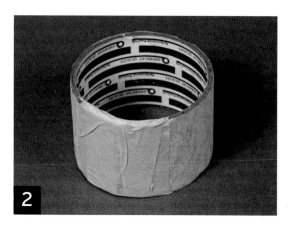

2 Rejoin the ends of the ring with masking tape.

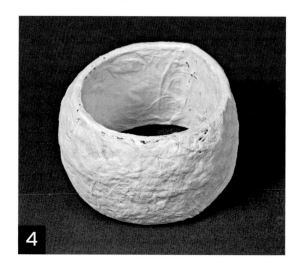

3 Apply papier mâché pulp to the inside and outside of the ring. Gently apply wallpaper paste with the palm of your hand to smooth it. When applying the pulp to the outside of the ring, make the middle a little thicker than the edges. Set it aside to dry for four or five days.

4 Apply a base coat of white acrylic paint to the bangle and set it aside to dry. Be sure to paint the outside and inside of the bangle.

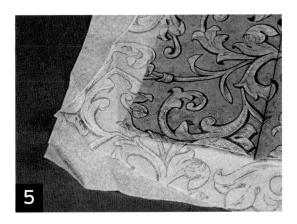

5 To prepare the decoupage, separate the sheets of a decorative napkin so that you are working with the printed sheet only.

6 Cut the printed sheet into strips that are about 1" (2.5 cm) wider than the bangle for laying on the outside of the bangle. Cut sheets that are the same width as the bangle for laying on the inside of the bangle.

7 Lay the wider strips on the outside of the bangle, taking care that they lie flat and overlap evenly on both sides.

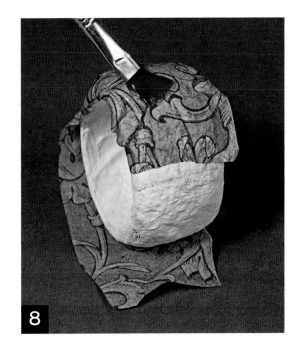

8 Use a paintbrush to apply wallpaper paste, brushing it from the center of the bangle outwards in order to press out crinkles and air pockets.

9 Lay the narrower strips on the inside of the bangle, and brush them with wallpaper paste. Set it aside to dry.

Something for Safekeeping

Final dimensions: 3" x 3" x 3" (7.6 x 7.6 x 7.6 cm)

Upgrade an ordinary box by covering it with a delicate layer of papier mâché pulp and adding splashes of acrylic paint. Decorate the box with beads, buttons, fancy lids, and anything else you like by pressing the decorative items into the wet pulp.

MATERIALS

- 3" x 3" x 2" (7.6 x 7.6 x 5 cm) box with lid
- pencil
- papier mâché pulp (see page 10)
- acrylic paints and paintbrushes
- varnish

Instructions

1 Put the lid on the box and trace the bottom edge of the lid on to the box. Apply papier mâché pulp to the area below this line—be careful that there is no pulp above the line, as this would prevent the box from closing properly. Turn the box over and apply papier mâché pulp to the bottom as well. Set it aside to dry for four or five days.

2 Apply papier mâché pulp to the lid. Form a ball of papier mâché pulp on the center of the lid. Form several small balls of papier mâché pulp at regular intervals along the sides of the lid. Set it aside to dry for three or four days.

3 When the box and lid are completely dry, apply a base coat of white acrylic paint. Allow the base coat to dry, then paint as desired. Apply a coat of varnish to finish.

Retro Beads

Final dimensions: 1"-3" (2.5-7.6 cm)

Follow these simple steps to make distinct, lightweight beads that can be used for necklaces, earrings, bracelets, or any other type of jewelry. Make a large batch of beads at one time and paint them at leisure, to suit any style or color scheme you like.

MATERIALS

· papier mâché pulp (see page 10)

· wallpaper paste

· wooden skewer

· plastic bowl

· acrylic paints and paintbrushes

· elastic beading string

· assorted beads

Instructions

1 Wet your hands and form balls of various sizes with the papier mâché pulp. Gently apply wallpaper paste with the palm of your hand to smooth the pulp as you work.

2 Carefully insert wooden skewers through the middle of each bead. Prop the skewers horizontally on a bowl rim and set them aside to dry for two or three days. Twist the skewers inside the beads periodically as they dry so that they don't get stuck inside.

3 Leave the beads on the skewers and apply a base coat of white acrylic paint. Set them aside to dry, and rotate the beads now and then as they dry so that the paint doesn't stick to the skewers.

4 Paint stripes, circles, and other patterns onto the beads. Set them aside to dry completely.

5 Tie a knot at the end of the thread and string on the papier mâché beads, integrating other beads as desired. Tie a knot at the other end, then tie the ends together.

Mobile of Love

Length: 30" (77 cm)

Is there any better way to say "I Love You" than with a handmade mobile of hearts? This piece is lovely for decorating a doorway, bedpost, or mirror.

MATERIALS

- papier mâché pulp (see page 10)
- wallpaper paste
- wooden skewers
- acrylic paints and paintbrushes
- nylon string
- assorted beads

Instructions

1 Sculpt birds and hearts in various sizes using the papier mâché pulp. Gently apply wallpaper paste with the palm of your hand to smooth them.

2 Carefully press a wooden skewer through the middle of each shape, from top to bottom. Take extra care when inserting skewers through the hearts so as not to pierce through the front or back. Skewer hearts and birds separately.

3 Set them aside to dry for three or four days. Lay the heart skewers flat to dry, and rotate them periodically. Lay the bird skewers across the rim of a bowl so that they are exposed to air all around. Twist the skewers inside the figures periodically so that the pulp doesn't stick.

4 When the shapes are completely dry, apply a base coat of white acrylic paint. It is easier to paint evenly if you leave the shapes on the skewers. Allow the base coat to dry, then paint as desired. Apply a coat of varnish. Set them aside to dry then remove shapes from skewers.

5 Tie a knot at one end of the string, string on some beads, then tie another knot. Leave some space on the string, and tie another knot. String on a papier mâché heart, then tie another knot. Continue in this manner, stringing beads and papier mâché shapes onto the string, leaving spaces here and there. Tie intermittent knots to separate the shapes so that each one is visible on its own.